My Very First
Canadian
Oxford
Dictionary

My name is

'For Rose, Amy and Eleanor' — C.K.

OXFORD
UNIVERSITY PRESS

70 Wynford Drive, Don Mills, Ontario, M3C 1J9 www.oup.com/ca

Oxford University Press is a department of the University of Oxford.
It furthers the University's objective of excellence in research, scholarship,
and education by publishing worldwide in

Oxford New York

Athens Auckland Bangkok Bogotá Buenos Aires Cape Town
Chennai Dar es Salaam Delhi Florence Hong Kong Istanbul Kolkata
Karachi Kuala Lumpur Madrid Melbourne Mexico City Mumbai
Nairobi Paris São Paulo Shanghai Singapore Taipei Tokyo Toronto Warsaw

With associated companies in
Berlin Ibadan

Oxford is a registered trade mark of Oxford University Press in the UK and in certain other countries

Published in Canada
by Oxford University Press
based on My Very First Oxford Dictionary published 1999

National Library of Canada Cataloguing in Publication Data

Kirtley, Clare

My very first Canadian Oxford dictionary

ISBN 0-19-541797-6

1. English language—Dictionaries, Juvenile. I. Bisset, Elizabeth II. Birkett, Georgie III. Title.

PE1628.5.K57 2002   j423   C2002-901148-5

1 2 3 4 – 05 04 03 02

Typeset in Gill Sans Schoolbook

Printed in China

My Very First Canadian Oxford Dictionary

Compiled by Clare Kirtley

Edited by Elizabeth Bisset

Illustrated by Georgie Birkett

OXFORD

UNIVERSITY PRESS

Contents

Introduction   6

A-Z dictionary   8

Words we write a lot   50

Verbs   52

Colours   56

Shapes   57

Days of the week   58

Months of the year   59

Numbers   60

The alphabet   62

Introduction

My Very First Canadian Oxford Dictionary helps young children enjoy and discover the features of a dictionary. It contains over 300 words in alphabetical order, each with a simple definition and a colourful picture. There are also additional end sections with words that children will find useful when writing. The words have been chosen to support and develop speaking, reading, and writing.

Here are the main features on the **A** to **Z** pages:

alphabet

capital letter

letter

symbol for verb

picture

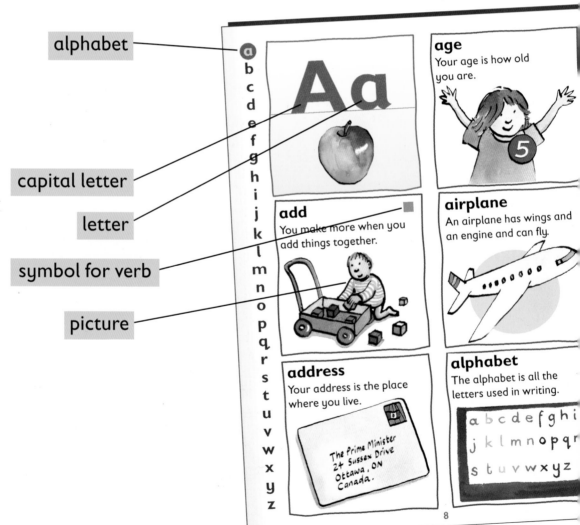

age
Your age is how old you are.

add
You make more when you add things together.

airplane
An airplane has wings and an engine and can fly.

address
Your address is the place where you live.

The Prime Minister
24 Sussex Drive
Ottawa, ON
Canada.

alphabet
The alphabet is all the letters used in writing.

a b c d e f g h i
j k l m n o p q r
s t u v w x y z

a b c d e f g h i j k l m n o p q r s t u v w x y z

8

My Very First Canadian Oxford Dictionary is an ideal introduction to dictionaries and other alphabetically ordered reference books. It helps children acquire basic dictionary and reference skills in a simple and enjoyable way: they can learn about the alphabet and about alphabetical order; they can find out how to locate a word by using the initial letter; they can check their own spelling; and they can learn how to use simple definitions of words.

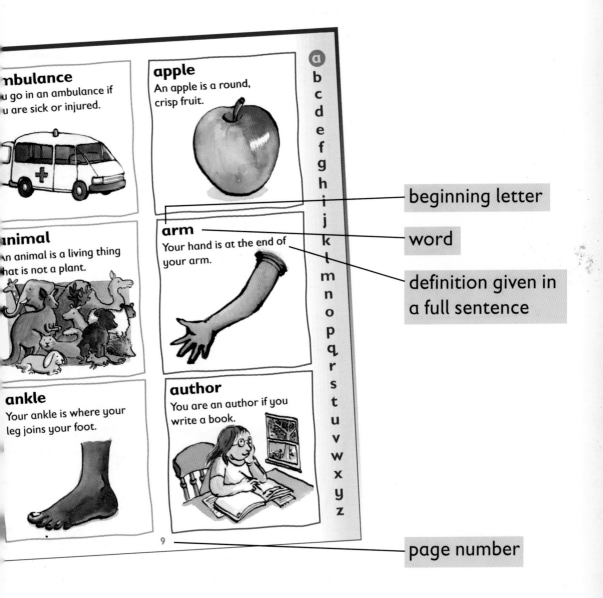

mbulance
u go in an ambulance if
u are sick or injured.

apple
An apple is a round,
crisp fruit.

animal
An animal is a living thing
hat is not a plant.

arm
Your hand is at the end of
your arm.

ankle
Your ankle is where your
leg joins your foot.

author
You are an author if you
write a book.

a b c d e f g h i j k l m n o p q r s t u v w x y z

beginning letter

word

definition given in
a full sentence

9

page number

Aa

age
Your age is how old you are.

add
You make more when you add things together.

airplane
An airplane has wings and an engine and can fly.

address
Your address is the place where you live.

The Prime Minister
24 Sussex Drive
Ottawa, ON
Canada.

alphabet
The alphabet is all the letters used in writing.

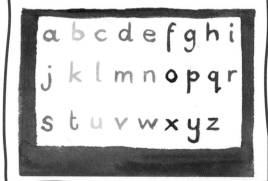

a b c d e f g h i
j k l m n o p q r
s t u v w x y z

ambulance

You go in an ambulance if you are sick or injured.

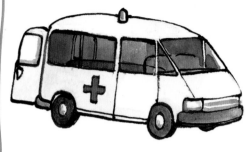

apple

An apple is a round, crisp fruit.

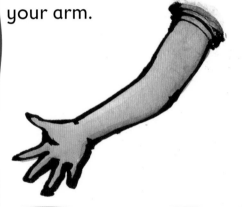

animal

An animal is a living thing that is not a plant.

arm

Your hand is at the end of your arm.

ankle

Your ankle is where your leg joins your foot.

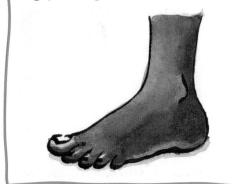

author

You are an author if you write a book.

a
b
c
d
e
f
g
h
i
j
k
l
m
n
o
p
q
r
s
t
u
v
w
x
y
z

Bb

bear
A bear is a big furry animal.

ball
A ball is round. You can play games with it.

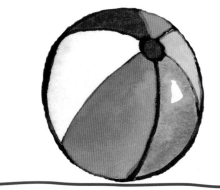

beaver
A beaver is an animal with a large tail. It builds dams.

banana
A banana is a long yellow fruit.

bed
You sleep in a bed.

bicycle
A bicycle has two wheels. You ride a bicycle.

book
A book has pages and a cover.

big
If something is big it is large.

bread
You make bread with flour and bake it in the oven.

bird
A bird has wings, feathers and a beak.

bus
A bus can carry lots of people.

a
b
c
d
e
f
g
h
i
j
k
l
m
n
o
p
q
r
s
t
u
v
w
x
y
z

Cc

canoe

A canoe is a small boat that you paddle.

cake

A cake is a sweet food.

car

A car has wheels and an engine.

camera

You take photos with a camera.

cat

A cat is a small furry animal.

chair

You sit on a chair.

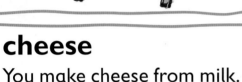

computer

A computer stores information.

cheese

You make cheese from milk.

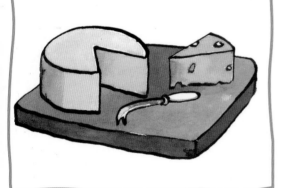

cow

A cow is a farm animal that gives milk.

clock

A clock tells you the time.

cup

You drink things from a cup.

a b **c** d e f g h i j k l m n o p q r s t u v w x y z

a b **c** d e f g h i j k l m n o p q r s t u v w x y z

Dd

dime

A dime is a coin worth ten cents.

dance

You move to music when you dance.

dinosaur

A dinosaur is an animal that lived a long time ago.

day

It is light during the day.

doctor

A doctor makes you better if you are sick.

14

dog
You can keep a dog as a pet.

dress
A girl sometimes wears a dress.

doll
A doll is a toy person.

drink ■
You can drink milk.

door
You open a door to go into a room.

duck
A duck is a bird that likes water.

a b c **d** e f g h i j k l m n o p q r s t u v w x y z

a b c d e f g h i j k l m n o p q r s t u v w x y z

Ee

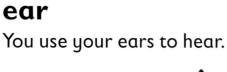

eat
You need to eat food to live.

ear
You use your ears to hear.

egg
A bird lives inside an egg before it hatches.

earth
You live on the planet Earth.

elbow
You bend your arm at your elbow.

electricity

You use electricity to get light and heat.

envelope

You put a letter in an envelope.

elephant

An elephant has a long nose called a trunk.

exercise

You need to exercise to keep fit.

empty

If something is empty it has nothing in it.

eye

You use your eyes to see.

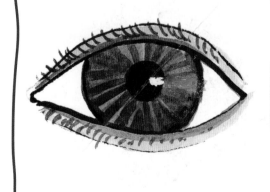

a b c d **e** f g h i j k l m n o p q r s t u v w x y z

Ff

farm

A farm is where food is grown.

fairy

You can read about a fairy in stories.

feather

Birds have feathers instead of fur or hair.

fall

You come down quickly when you fall.

fish

A fish lives under water.

flag

A flag is a piece of cloth on a pole. The Canadian flag has a red maple leaf on it.

fox

A fox is a wild animal with a furry tail.

foot

Your foot is at the end of your leg.

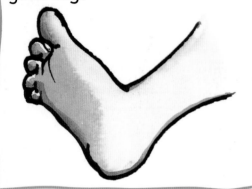

frog

A frog has wet skin and webbed feet.

fork

You use a fork to eat.

fruit

You can eat fruit. Apples and oranges are fruit.

Gg

garden
You can grow flowers and vegetables in a garden.

game
You play a game.

gate
A gate is an outside door.

garbage
When something isn't useful anymore you put it into the garbage.

giant
A giant is a very big person.

giraffe

A giraffe has a long neck.

good

If something is good you like it.

glass

A window is made of glass.

grow

Things get bigger when they grow.

glue

You use glue to stick things together.

guitar

A guitar is an instrument with strings.

a b c d e f g h i j k l m n o p q r s t u v w x y z

Hh

head

Your eyes and ears are on your head.

hand

You hold things with your hand.

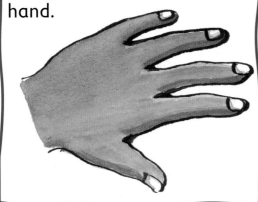

hill

A hill is a piece of high land.

hat

You wear a hat on your head.

hockey

Hockey is a game you play on ice.

holiday

A holiday is when you do not go to school or work.

hot

If something is hot it can burn you.

horse

You can ride a horse.

house

You can live in a house.

hospital

You go to the hospital when you are sick.

hungry

If you are hungry you want to eat.

a b c d e f g **h** i j k l m n o p q r s t u v w x y z

Ii

information

You use information to find out about things.

ice

Freezing water turns to ice.

insect

An insect is a small animal with six legs.

igloo

An igloo is a house made of snow.

instrument

You use an instrument to make music.

Jj

jug
You use a jug to pour a drink.

jam
You make jam from fruit and sugar.

juggler
A juggler throws things in the air and catches them.

journey
You travel from place to place on a journey.

jump
You go up into the air when you jump.

Kk

kettle

You use a kettle to boil water.

kangaroo

A kangaroo has big back legs and jumps.

key

You use a key to unlock a door.

keep

If you keep something you do not give it away.

kick

You kick a ball with your foot.

26

kind

You are being kind when you help other people.

kite

A kite flies in the air at the end of a long string.

king

Some countries are ruled by a king.

knee

Your knee is where your leg bends.

kitchen

You cook in a kitchen.

knife

You use a knife to cut things.

a b c d e f g h i j **k** l m n o p q r s t u v w x y z

Ll

leaf
A leaf grows on a plant.

ladybug
A ladybug is a small flying insect with spots.

leg
You use your legs to walk.

laugh
You laugh when something is funny.

letter
You use letters to write words.

library

Books are kept in a library.

little

If something is little it is not big.

like

If you like someone you think they are nice.

loonie

A loonie is a coin worth one dollar.

lion

A lion is a big wild cat.

loud

You can hear loud sounds easily.

a b c d e f g h i j k **l** m n o p q r s t u v w x y z

Mm

meat

We eat meat from animals.

make

You make something by putting things together.

metal

Something made of metal is hard.

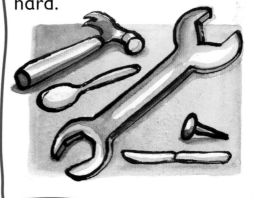

map

A map shows you how to get to places.

milk

You can drink cow's milk.

money

You use money to buy things.

moose

A moose is an animal with wide horns and a long nose.

monkey

A monkey is furry and lives in trees.

mountain

A mountain is a high hill.

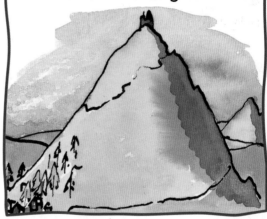

moon

You often see the moon in the sky at night.

mouth

You use your mouth to speak and eat.

a b c d e f g h i j k l m n o p q r s t u v w x y z

Nn

necklace

You wear a necklace around your neck.

name

Your name is what people call you.

nest

A bird lives in a nest.

neck

Your neck joins your head to your shoulders.

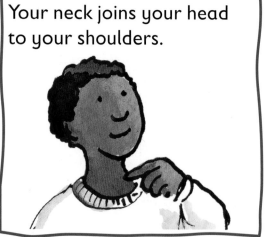

new

Something is new when you first get it.

nice

If something is nice you enjoy it.

noise

A noise is a loud sound.

nickel

A nickel is a coin worth five cents.

nose

You use your nose to smell.

night

It is dark at night time.

number

You use numbers to count.

a b c d e f g h i j k l m **n** o p q r s t u v w x y z

Oo

open

You can open a door.

octopus

An octopus has eight arms.

orange

An orange is a round fruit with thick peel.

old

You are old if you were born a long time ago.

owl

An owl is a bird who flies at night.

Pp

paper
You write on paper.

page
A page is part of a book.

park
You can play in a park.

pants
You wear pants on your legs.

pencil
You use a pencil to write or draw.

a b c d e f g h i j k l m n o **p** q r s t u v w x y z

penny

A penny is a coin worth one cent.

plant

A plant grows out of the ground.

piano

A piano is an instrument with black and white keys.

plate

You put food on a plate.

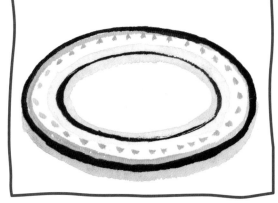

pig

A pig is a fat farm animal.

play

You have fun when you play.

Qq

question

You ask a question to find out something.

quarter

A quarter is a coin worth twenty-five cents.

quick

You are quick when you move fast.

queen

A queen is a woman who rules a country.

quiet

You are quiet when you make very little noise.

a b c d e f g h i j k l m n o p **q** r s t u v w x y z

Rr

rainbow

Sun shines through rain to make a rainbow.

rabbit

A rabbit is a small animal with long ears.

read

You read books, cards and letters.

rain

The rain is water falling from the sky.

recorder

A recorder is an instrument that you blow.

rhinoceros

A rhinoceros has a horn on its nose.

robot

A robot is a machine that moves like a person.

river

A river is a large stream of water.

rocket

A rocket sends spacecraft into space.

road

Cars and buses travel on a road.

run

You move your legs quickly to run.

a b c d e f g h i j k l m n o p q **r** s t u v w x y z

Ss

seed

A plant grows from a seed.

school

You go to school to learn.

sheep

You get wool from a sheep.

scissors

You use scissors to cut things.

shirt

A shirt has sleeves and a collar.

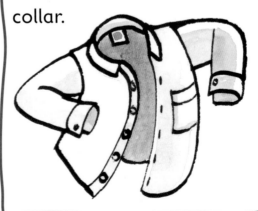

shoe

You wear a shoe on your foot.

store

You buy things in a store.

snow

Snow falls when it is cold.

story

A story tells you about something that has happened.

sock

You wear a sock on your foot.

sun

It is warm and bright in the sun.

a b c d e f g h i j k l m n o p q r s t u v w x y z

Tt

teeth

You use your teeth to bite.

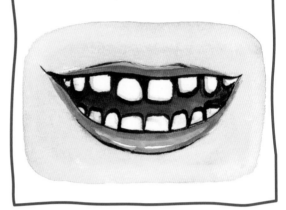

table

You sit at a table.

telephone

You use a telephone to speak to people.

teacher

A teacher helps you to learn.

television

You watch and listen to things on television.

toonie

A toonie is a coin worth two dollars.

toy

You play with a toy.

toque

A toque is a hat you wear in the winter.

train

A train goes on a track.

towel

You use a towel to dry yourself.

tree

A tree is a tall plant with leaves.

a b c d e f g h i j k l m n o p q r s **t** u v w x y z

Uu

uniform

Some people wear a uniform to work or to school.

ugly

If something is ugly it is not nice to look at.

upset

You are not happy when you are upset.

umbrella

You use an umbrella to keep dry when it rains.

use

You use tools to make things.

a b c d e f g h i j k l m n o p q r s t **u** v w x y z

V v

vet

A vet is an animal doctor.

vase

You put flowers in a vase.

video

A video records sound and pictures from the television.

vegetable

A vegetable is a plant that you can eat.

violin

You play a violin with a bow.

Ww

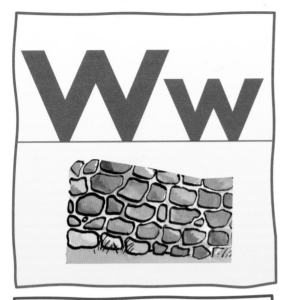

wind
The wind is air moving.

wall
A wall is made of brick or stone.

word
You use words when you speak or write.

water
Rivers and seas are made up of water.

write
You write words for other people to read.

Xx

Yy

X-ray

An X-ray shows the inside of your body.

yacht

A yacht is a boat with sails.

xylophone

A xylophone is an instrument with wooden bars.

yawn

You yawn when you are tired.

a b c d e f g h i j k l m n o p q r s t u v w x y z

year

There are twelve months in a year.

Zz

yogourt

You make yogourt from sour milk.

zebra

A zebra has black and white stripes.

young

You are young if you were born a short time ago.

zigzag

A zigzag line turns sharply.

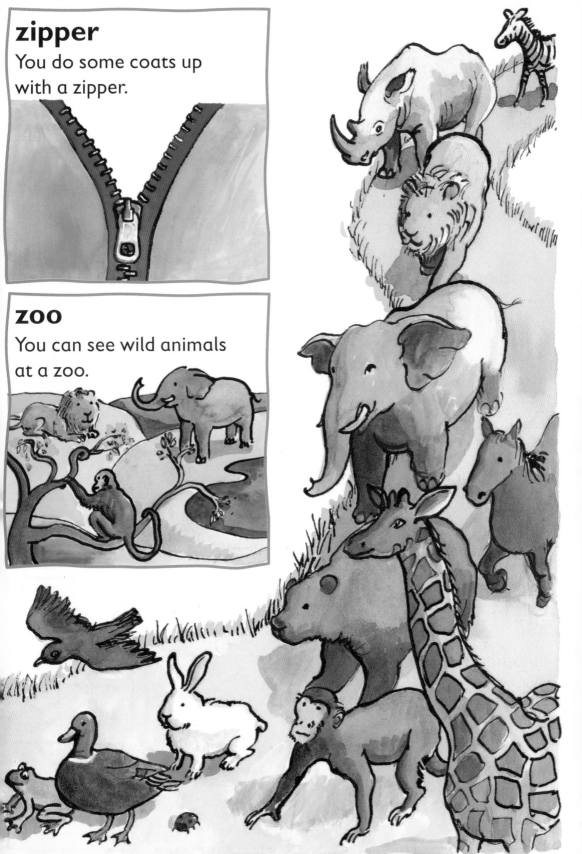

zipper

You do some coats up
with a zipper.

zoo

You can see wild animals
at a zoo.

a b c d e f g h i j k l m n o p q r s t u v w x y z

Words we write a lot

a
about
after
again
all
am
an
and
another
are
as
at
away

back
ball
be
because
bed
been
big
boy
brother
but
by

call
called
came
can
Canada
can't
cat
children
class
come
could
cross

dad
day
did
dig
do
dog
don't
door
down

eat
end
every
everyone

first
for
friend
from

get
girl
go
going
good
got

had
half
has
have
he
help
her
here
him
his
home
house
how

I
if
in
is
it

jump
just

last
laugh
like
liked
little
live
lived
look
looked
lots
love

made
make
man
many
may
me
mom
more
much
must
my

name	said	under	**Provinces and Territories**
new	saw	up	Alberta
next	school	us	British
night	see		Columbia
no	seen	very	Manitoba
not	she		New
now	should	want	Brunswick
	sick	was	Newfoundland
of	sister	water	Northwest
off	sit	way	Territories
old	so	we	Nova Scotia
on	some	went	Nunavut
once		were	Ontario
one	take	what	Prince Edward
or	than	when	Island
our	thank	where	Quebec
out	that	who	Saskatchewan
over	the	why	Yukon
	their	will	Territory
people	them	with	
play	then	woman	
please	there	would	
pull	these		
pulled	they	yes	
push	this	you	
put	three	your	
	time		
ran	to		
	too		
	took		
	tree		
	two		

Verbs (These are doing words)

add

carry

cry

bounce

catch

clap

cut

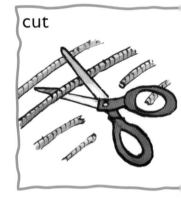

buy

climb

dance

call

cook

dig

drink

grow

keep

eat

hear

kick

exercise

help

laugh

hop

fall

jump

like

More verbs

listen

paint

run

look

play

see

pull

make

push

sing

open

read

sit

sleep

talk

walk

smell

taste

wash

throw

smile

write

touch

take

use

yawn

Colours

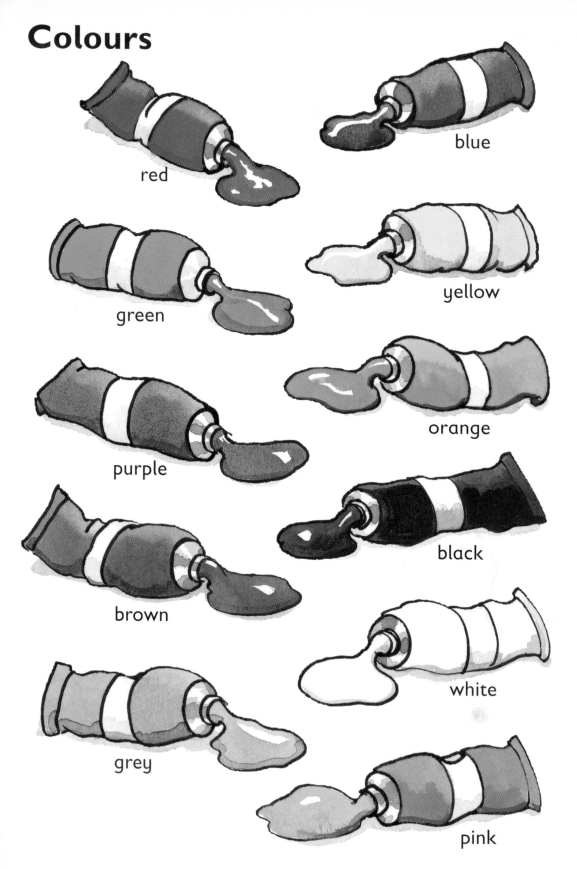

red

blue

green

yellow

purple

orange

brown

black

grey

white

pink

Shapes

square

triangle

circle

rectangle

Days of the week

Sunday

Monday

Saturday

Tuesday

Friday

Wednesday

Thursday

Months of the year

January

February

March

April

May

June

July

August

September

October

November

December

Numbers

zero   **0**

one   **1**

two   **2**

three   **3**

four   **4**

five   **5**

six   **6**

seven   **7**

eight   **8**

nine   **9**

ten **10**

eleven **11**

twelve **12**

thirteen **13**

fourteen **14**

fifteen **15**

sixteen **16**

seventeen **17**

eighteen **18**

nineteen **19**

twenty **20**

The alphabet

A a

B b

C c

D d

E e

F f

G g

H h

I i

J j

K k

L l

Mm		**Tt**	
Nn		**Uu**	
Oo		**Vv**	
Pp		**Ww**	
Qq		**Xx**	
Rr		**Yy**	
Ss		**Zz**